the guide to owning a
Lovebird

David E. Boruchowitz

© **T.F.H. Publications, Inc.**

Distributed in the UNITED STATES to the Pet Trade by T.F.H. Publications, Inc., 1 TFH Plaza, Neptune City, NJ 07753; on the Internet at www.tfh.com; in CANADA by Rolf C. Hagen Inc., 3225 Sartelon St., Montreal, Quebec H4R 1E8; Pet Trade by H & L Pet Supplies Inc., 27 Kingston Crescent, Kitchener, Ontario N2B 2T6; in ENGLAND by T.F.H. Publications, PO Box 74, Havant PO9 5TT; in AUSTRALIA AND THE SOUTH PACIFIC by T.F.H. (Australia), Pty. Ltd., Box 149, Brookvale 2100 N.S.W., Australia; in NEW ZEALAND by Brooklands Aquarium Ltd., 5 McGiven Drive, New Plymouth, RD1 New Zealand; in SOUTH AFRICA by Rolf C. Hagen S.A. (PTY.) LTD., P.O. Box 201199, Durban North 4016, South Africa; in Japan by T.F.H. Publications. Published by T.F.H. Publications, Inc.

Contents

In Love
With Lovebirds

Lovebirds are colorful African parrots that have remained popular because of their affordability and availability; the Peachfaced is the most commonly kept lovebird.

The tiny parrots of the genus *Agapornis* are especially lovable little pets. They are colorful, garrulous, fun-loving birds, and what they lack in size, they make up for in spunk and curiosity. Although your lovebird's chatting ability is unlikely ever to put an Amazon or African Grey parrot to shame, it might learn to squeak a few words or to whistle a few notes, and it will definitely return the love and care you give it with an affectionate, comical personality.

This book will introduce you to all of the species, with special attention to the three most common in aviculture. You'll learn all you need to know to select, house, feed, train, and care for your own lovebird.

WHAT IS A LOVEBIRD?

The name lovebird is applied to the different species in the genus *Agapornis,* a group of diminutive African parrots. Imagine shrinking a full-sized parrot to about 6 inches long—that's a lovebird.

No One Told Them

An apt description of these little clowns is that no one ever told them they weren't "real" parrots. They are bold and curious, and they act very much like large parrots. The major difference in their behavior is that they do not hold and manipulate objects in their feet, using them as hands, the way all larger parrots do.

You may consider it either an asset or a liability, but lovebirds *sound* a bit like large parrots. I still remember my delight with my very first pair of lovebirds three decades ago, and my glee when I heard their jungle cries. I marveled that such a tiny bird could make so large and wild a sound. Though it lacks the depth and volume of the screech of an Amazon or a cockatoo, the call of a lovebird is definitely exotic-sounding and not at all like the chittering of budgies or the warbling of finches.

Where Do They Come From?

There are nine species of lovebirds, and they are all African, with one of them, *Agapornis cana*, coming from the African island nation of Madagascar. They inhabit savannah and wooded areas and are never found far from water.

What Do They Look Like?

Though it is true to say that all lovebirds are basically green, this fails miserably to capture the striking beauty of these birds. It does, however, explain the common names used for these animals, since for the most part they make mention of the other coloration on the birds. One look at the pictures in this book, and you will see what I mean about their striking beauty. There are slight differences in size among

A lovebird's small size—about six inches—makes it a good pet for nearly any living situation, from city apartment to country farm.

the species, but they are all 5 to 6 inches long. Since their tail is short and wide, this means that they are a very stocky bird, compared to, say, a budgie, whose length is about half tail.

Unusual Breeding Habits

The genus *Agapornis* contains some very unusual parrots—unusual in the sense that they build nests. Almost all parrots simply nest in cavities, usually in trees, and they do not collect nesting material; instead they just lay their eggs on the wood chips that line the nesting hole. The most nest preparation they do is to chew up the wood inside the hole, throw some out, and make a depression in what's left for the eggs.

Some lovebirds, on the other hand, look for, cut, and transport strips of vegetation with which they line their nest cavities. Some build rather elaborate nests. But there's more—some species of lovebirds have developed the ability to carry this nesting material tucked in their feathers, so that a hen on her way to the nest looks like she's been decorated with streamers.

Lovebirds cut the nesting material into distinctive strips, long and thin. They follow the contours of the material most of the time, meaning they can wind up with curved or even L-shaped pieces. Although they use large leaves in the wild, captive lovebirds will use various materials for their nests. They will use newspaper, but they prefer something a bit heavier. I've found that brown paper grocery bags make excellent material.

SCIENTIFIC NOTATION

Back in the 1960s, the ethologist William Dilger did an extensive study of the genetic basis for the nest material transport behavior of lovebirds and made many significant findings. For example, Masked Lovebirds carry a single strip of nesting material in their beaks, but Peachfaced Lovebirds carry several strips at a time, tucking them into the feathers of the rump. Hybrid birds try to tuck the strips into their feathers, but they fail to let go, so the strip stays in the beak, and they drop it. After several years of this futile behavior, they can learn to carry the strips successfully, but even then they still twist their head back as if to tuck the strip before they fly with the strip in their beak. Thus, although there is a strong genetic (instinctive) component to this behavior, the birds can learn to modify it through trial and error.

Caring for a Lovebird

It is not difficult to provide the proper care for a lovebird, but it is a serious responsibility. You must, of course, be committed to the care of any pet, but with a bird as friendly and as intelligent as a lovebird, that care includes a lot of time beyond just providing a clean cage and food and water. Fortunately, that time will be very enjoyable for you, because it involves playing with your pet and taking care of its emotional needs.

AN INTELLIGENT PET

Emotional needs? That's right, all parrots, including lovebirds, are intelligent and social creatures. The very name "lovebird" comes from the fact that these birds form such close bonds with each other; in French they are called *les inséparables*—"the inseparable ones." They do form tight bonds early in life, and many people think you must keep them in pairs.

Like any parrot, a lovebird requires personal attention and companionship from its owner in order to thrive. Pictured is the Fischer's Lovebird.

If, however, you get a handfed bird and keep it by itself, it will come to bond the same way with you, and it will want to be your constant companion. This is the most enjoyable thing about owning a tame bird, but it means that you must be prepared to spend a lot of time with the bird and provide it with enough stimulation (read: toys) that it does not get bored. A bored bird may develop bad habits like plucking its own feathers.

TOYS

Too many people have the image of a bird sitting on a perch in a cage and twittering to itself all day. This isn't even accurate for a canary or a finch, but for hookbills (parrots and parakeets), it is a horrible representation. Even if you keep more than one lovebird, toys are essential to keep them entertained.

Your pet store will have a large assortment of bird toys that are safe. Especially to be avoided are toys with loops or holes in which the bird could get its head, wing, or toes caught. A little lovebird's beak is not able to destroy toys the way a large parrot can, but whittling and biting are important to keeping any parrot's beak in shape, so you must be sure to provide wooden toys (or even little blocks of scrap wood) for them to chew on. Lovebirds are active acrobats and will greatly appreciate playing on swings, ladders, ropes, chains, and other climbing apparatus. Remember to change the bird's toys often to prevent boredom. This does not mean you have to buy a new toy once a week. Simply rotate them regularly, and, as with a toddler, the old toys that have been stored for a while will seem "new."

THE CAGE

Your lovebird's cage must be clean, safe, and comfortable. It should have a slide-

Toys and other amusements are essential to your lovebird's happiness; a bored lovebird may turn to bad habits such as screeching or feather plucking.

A cage should be large enough for a bird to fly around in and exercise, so plan to buy the largest cage you can afford.

out tray at the bottom to make cleaning easy and quick. Newspaper is probably the best thing you can use to line the tray. It is cheap and effective, and it is safe for the bird to chew up into confetti—which it will do!

The best arrangement is to have a wire floor above the tray, so that the bird does not have access to it. This is easier said than done, however, and often a persistent bird can get to the newspaper anyway. Since the various litter materials sometimes used in bird cages have been implicated in impactions of the digestive system in pet birds, it is safer to avoid using them and stick with the newspaper. By changing the paper daily, you will not only keep your bird clean and healthy, you will be able to monitor its droppings. Since a change in the quantity, texture, or color of a bird's droppings is often the first symptom of a health problem, it is important to know what they are normally like and to identify immediately if they change significantly. There will, of course, be some variation with the diet. For example, extra fruits or greens may

Cage bar spacing and direction are important details to consider, especially for birds like lovebirds that tend to climb up and down.

cause looser stools, and feeding a highly colored food like beets or berries can cause a temporary change in their color.

Buy a cage that has bar spacing suited to lovebirds. You probably won't find one made specifically for lovebirds, but a cage designed for budgies would be fine. This means that the bars are close enough together so the bird cannot get its head through the wire. It also means that at least part of the cage will have horizontal bars so that your bird can climb easily. Lovebirds climb with a beak-over-feet motion, and it is difficult for them to do on vertically placed bars. Any doors should latch securely, because lovebirds often figure out how to lift and open unlatched doors.

How big should the cage be? This is a case of the bigger, the better. Lovebirds do very well in large outdoor aviaries, 16 feet long or more. They don't *need* such giant accommodations, though they do

Perches, whether purchased from a store or made from natural branches, should be clean and safe for birds to chew on.

enjoy them. At the very least, the cage should be large enough so the bird can fly from one end to the other. It is cruel to confine a bird as active as a lovebird to a cage so small it can merely hop from perch to perch. Of course, a lovebird is not very large, so a 24-inch cage provides ample room for it to fly. If you allow the bird some time outside the cage every day, a smaller cage can suffice, because your pet will get plenty of flying exercise when it is free in the room.

Perches

There are many types of perches available—wood, plastic, braided rope, natural, and even concrete for keeping toenails and beaks trimmed. The important thing is to have perches of

FREE TIME

Allowing your bird to fly free in your home is a great way to give it exercise and to spend time with it. As long as it is tame and will step up onto your finger, it is safe to allow it to have free time while you are there to keep an eye on it. You will need to make sure that you have bird-proofed the room, extinguishing open flames, and closing doors, windows, toilet seats, cabinets, and other potential escape routes or dangers. Your bird will enjoy a bird playpen. These are made of wood or plastic and often fit on top of a bird's cage. They contain climbing and other toys and usually offer food and water dishes as well as a bottom tray for easy cleanup.

different diameters, so that the bird's feet get natural exercise and variety. My personal preference is to use natural branches. Aside from being non-uniform in size, they offer twigs and bark for the birds to chew on, which they love to do. If you have a place where you can gather natural branches, this is ideal, but make sure that the trees you select are not poisonous to your bird and have not been sprayed with insecticides. Safe trees include maple, willow, and fruit trees. Pieces of grapevine are perfect, and the birds love chewing off the coarse bark. Although standard kiln-dried lumber, which is fir or pine, is fine for birds to chew, do not use natural pine branches, because the fresh sap can be detrimental, not to mention sticky and messy.

Food and Water Cups

You have two choices for water: a dirty bowl or a water bottle. I say that because no matter how hard you try, a water bowl will usually be dirty with seed hulls, bits of food, pieces of paper, and bird droppings. It is easy to train a lovebird to drink from a bottle. They are naturally curious, and if you buy a bottle specifically made for birds, it will probably have a bright red regulator ball in the tube, which is usually sufficient to attract the bird's attention. Once the bird has poked the ball and gotten a drop of water, it will know where to get a drink. Just watch to be certain it is drinking.

Do not simply fill the bottle and forget about it. Every day, when you clean the cage, you should tap or squeeze the

Keep a secure travel cage on hand for vacations as well as emergencies, and always bring along food, water, and treats.

Preening is your bird's way of maintaining healthy feathers, which are essential for flight and insulation from the cold.

bottle to make sure a drop comes out, and every few days you must take it off the cage and clean it thoroughly. In fact, I recommend having two bottles and rotating them, letting each dry completely after you clean it. This helps prevent bacteria from growing in it. A mild chlorine bleach solution is excellent for sterilizing the bottle after washing it in soapy water. Make sure you rinse all soap and disinfectant from the bottle, then let it dry. You can buy a special brush designed to clean both the bottle and the drinking tube.

Food bowls, especially those used for moist foods, must also be cleaned and disinfected regularly, and it helps to have two sets so you can rotate them also. Some lovebirds insist on dumping their food bowls; if yours develops this annoying habit, you can purchase special bowls that lock to the side of the cage and that will thwart the most determined bowl-dumper. There is really no advantage to either the bowls that sit on the floor of the cage or cups that attach to the bars—choose whichever you prefer.

BATHS

Almost all lovebirds come from dry habitats, but they are always found close

THE GUIDE TO OWNING A LOVEBIRD

to water holes, where they gather in flocks to bathe. Most pet lovebirds also love to bathe, and it helps them keep their feathers in perfect condition. Often they enjoy being misted with a small spray bottle full of water. Some will even get into the shower with their human friends! You can provide any or all of these opportunities. If your bird clearly objects to getting wet, it is not necessary to force the issue, but you could try again a few weeks later to see if the idea has gained in appeal. Just make sure that whenever your bird bathes by any means, it has a warm, dry, draft-free spot to completely dry its feathers afterwards. There it will preen itself until it is dry and all of its feathers are back in place.

PREENING

Preening is a type of care a bird does for itself, but you should be aware of its purpose and importance. Feathers are remarkable things, and they are crucial to a bird's survival. Only an extremely sick bird will allow its feathers to become disarrayed. Even very young birds preen themselves; by the time their feathers grow in, they are already preening, and the parents do not have to do this for

Preening and feeding are two social acts commonly seen among lovebirds.

them. Aside from carrying the bird's coloration, which they use to recognize their own kind, feathers serve two very important functions—insulation and flight.

Because they are hollow and fit together in an overlapping fashion, a bird's feathers trap air and provide excellent insulation. In addition, their coating of oil makes them water-resistant, keeping the bird dry.

Of course, feathers are an enormous advantage for flight. They are aerodynamically ideal, and the fact that the bird can change their orientation with special muscles enables it to perform precise aerial maneuvers.

Because of their importance for survival, a bird spends a good deal of its time preening its feathers. Feathers have a barb-and-hook design, which keeps the many independent fronds locked into an integral whole. When they are brushed the wrong way, the fronds unhook, but by pulling them through its beak, a bird can rehook them, maintaining their proper shape. At the same time, by periodically dipping its bill into the oil gland located at the base of the tail on the back, the bird can coat each feather with the oil in order to maintain its waterproofing.

Watch a bird when it is preening and you will see it take each feather shaft in its beak in turn, sliding the beak down the feather from base to tip, locking all the barbs together. It will often reach back to the oil gland, then rub its beak on its feathers, spreading the oil through them.

Lovebirds spend a lot of time preening each other, so don't be surprised if your pet tries to preen your hair! Aside from helping to reach places like the back of their head, this type of social preening strengthens the bonds between the birds. A pair of lovebirds will often sit close together on a perch, preening and feeding each other. Tame pets often enjoy sitting on their owner's head, shoulder, or even eyeglasses.

SUNLIGHT

Like most animals, lovebirds need vitamin D, and like most animals, they can synthesize vitamin D when they are exposed to the ultraviolet rays of the sun. Since these do not penetrate window glass, unless your lovebird spends time in a wired or screened enclosure outside, it will need a source of vitamin D in its diet. Commercial pellets are fortified with this and other vitamins, and it can be found in other food items, such as milk products.

Many people are convinced that full spectrum lighting is important to birds in other ways, and they keep their birds under special bulbs that imitate the natural light of the sun. Others, however, find that their birds do fine without this. In any case, it is clear that sunlight is a great stimulus for birds, and your lovebird will probably greet both sunrise and sunset with excited vocalizations. In addition, most birds will respond to direct sunlight (or a similar source such as a hot light bulb) by "sunbathing," stretching their wings, and obviously enjoying themselves.

All this talk of sunlight might suggest the possibility of taking your pet lovebird outside with you. This, however, is a very risky thing to do.

PLAYING OUTSIDE

There are many factors to consider about outside time for your bird. If your bird has not had the feathers on its wings clipped to curtail its flying ability, it is very likely that you will lose it. Even a snugly bird that flies to you whenever you call and never wants to get off your head or shoulder stands a good chance of disappearing if you take it outside. Pet birds are accustomed to life indoors and have no experience navigating under the open sky. Spurred by curiosity or spooked by some strange noise or sight, it will bolt skyward and soon be out of sight, with no idea of how to get back or even where "back" is. Predators are also a constant threat. From a neighborhood cat or dog to various wild animals, there are many creatures that would love to have a lovebird for lunch.

You might think that you'll clip your bird's wings and then take it outside. Even then there is considerable risk. First of all, parrots are excellent climbers. A flightless lovebird can quickly disappear into the treetops by climbing. They also run very fast and can lead you on quite a chase across the lawn. You may be sure your pet will stay close to you, but there are so many scary sights and sounds outside that your bird is not accustomed to that its deep-rooted instinct to flee may very well overcome its bond to you.

What about time outside, but in a cage? This is a possibility, but again, you must take special precautions. For example, many birdcages consist of a plastic base with slots in it, into which tabs in the cage fit. These can easily separate, with the bottom literally dropping out. Sliding cage doors without latches can open unintentionally, and some latches are gravity-dependent and may open up if the cage is tipped the wrong way.

A cage provides protection from household dangers such as ceiling fans, open toilets, and cats or other pets.

A large flight cage made of welded wire mesh, into which your lovebird is placed while still inside the house, and which has all its doors wired shut, can be used to provide your pet with time outside in the sun and fresh air. You must never leave the bird unattended outside, however.

The first danger is from overheating. A bird in the direct sun can quickly succumb, and a shady spot rapidly becomes a sunny one as the day progresses.

Even in a secure cage, your bird is at risk from such predators as large dogs, and no cage is secure enough to protect your pet from theft or harm by human predators.

Last but not least, a bird outside is in danger of disease spread by wild birds. Many avian diseases are spread in bird droppings, and wild birds may perch on the outside of the cage, exposing your lovebird. They may also shed parasites such as lice and mites, which your bird might pick up.

Feeding Lovebirds

The area of bird nutrition has undergone massive research, experimentation, and change in the last couple of decades. We now know that the old all-seed diet is woefully inadequate for parrots, and all this research has produced many excellent pelleted foods, which are available in many sizes, including ones suitable for lovebirds. There are also good seed mixes for lovebirds. These should be a mixture of white millet and canary seed and can have other seeds added. Sunflower seeds are really treats, being too fatty for everyday fare. Either use a mix with few sunflower seeds, or use one without any and offer sunflower seeds by themselves as a treat. (They are especially useful when taming and training your bird.) The foundation of your lovebird's diet can be either a quality seed mix or a specially formulated pellet, but in either case it should be supplemented.

Whatever food you give your lovebird should be provided in sturdy and clean containers or crocks.

FRUITS AND VEGGIES

If you base the diet on a seed mix, you should supplement with fruits and

When keeping several birds be certain you provide enough food for all; aggressive birds may make it difficult for timid birds to eat.

vegetables every day. With a pelleted diet you do not need to be so consistent, though there is no harm in offering these foods on a daily basis. You can feed your bird any fruit or vegetable suitable for human consumption *except avocados,* which are reported to be toxic to birds. The key is variety. Feed lots of different foods, taking advantage of what is in season. Especially nutritious are dark green leafy vegetables like chard or beet greens, parsley, kale, or spinach, and orange ones like carrots, yams, and squash. Raw vegetables have the most vitamins; they can be chopped or grated, or fed as whole pieces.

Remember that many "waste" items from your kitchen make excellent bird food—trimmings, tops, and seeds of many fruits and vegetables are suitable, including watermelon (rind and seeds), carrot tops, and the outer leaves of dark green lettuce. Do not feed iceberg lettuce, which nutritionally is little more than water. The seeds and insides that you remove from squash, pumpkins, or melons are a favorite of birds. When I place a bowl of cantaloupe scrapings in my lovebirds' cage, it is gone in no time. Most lovebirds are also extremely fond of corn on the cob.

Another good food is frozen vegetables. They should be thawed, but not cooked. Almost any vegetable is a good choice, but I lean heavily toward a frozen mix, because it automatically provides a nice variety of foods.

ANIMAL PROTEIN

It is extremely difficult to provide all of your lovebird's nutrition without using some animal protein, the same way it is very hard to meet all of our nutritional needs without using some animal products, whether meat, milk, or eggs. This can come from pellets, or you can supplement it in the diet.

Meat

In the wild, lovebirds eat some meat, in the form of insects, worms, grubs, and an occasional egg or small animal of some kind. You can offer your bird small portions of very lean, cooked poultry to provide the protein and vitamins they would otherwise lack in a vegetarian diet. Some people prefer to feed live foods such as mealworms, and many lovebirds enjoy these, while others will not touch them.

Milk

Liquid milk is not suitable for feeding your bird, but some cheeses are. Cottage cheese is a good choice, but regular hard cheeses are not, because of their high fat content. Low-fat versions of them are acceptable.

Eggs

I am a great proponent of feeding eggs to birds. Eggs contain all of the necessary nutrition to make a baby bird (if you include the shell as a source of calcium for bones). Their only drawback is that they are too rich and fatty to feed every day. I try to feed eggs about once a week, and the preferred method is to hard-boil the eggs, then use a sharp knife to slice them lengthwise in half, *without removing the shell.* Just place the half-eggs into the cage and watch your bird go crazy. I have never had a bird, from tiny finches to large parrots, from chickens to peacocks, from doves to turkeys, that didn't eat eggs excitedly. Remember to remove all fresh foods after a couple of hours so that they will not be eaten after they begin spoiling.

Other Foods

Grains and legumes of all kinds are ideal food for lovebirds. Brown rice, dry beans,

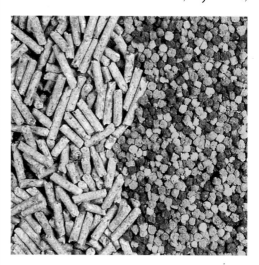

Pellets, which come in a wide array of sizes and colors, can form the foundation of a healthy diet; however, fresh fruits and vegetables should be added for variety.

Change your bird's food supply on a daily basis to prevent the buildup of empty seed hulls and shells.

and pasta can be cooked until tender and fed, either as is or mixed with vegetables or bread. Many people bake "birdy bread," which is simply a cornbread recipe with the addition of things such as sunflower seeds and green vegetables. Regular whole-grain breads are also relished by lovebirds and provide a lot of nutrition. Remember that the more variety you provide, the better the diet will be, and the more likely your pet will be to try new foods when you offer them, because rather than associating a particular food item with mealtime, it will consider anything you put into its food bowl as a proper meal.

Treats

Birds, like people, don't always like to eat what's good for them, and they very often do like to eat what isn't good for them. Caffeine (in coffee, tea, chocolate, or cola), salt, and an excess of sugar or fat should not be given to your bird. You must realize that when you consume these substances, the amount is quite small in relation to your total body mass, but even a small piece of chocolate or a little bit of nachos represents a substantial percent of your lovebird's mass.

So what are good treats? I've already mentioned a real favorite—sunflower seeds. Your bird will soon let you know which foods it particularly likes, and its favorite might be grapes or corn or graham crackers. One thing relished by almost all birds, from lovebirds to macaws, is spray millet. This is millet dried

CALCIUM

Birds need calcium, especially when breeding. Mineral blocks and cuttlebone are common sources, and eggshells are another good one. Whenever you use eggs to feed your bird, whether alone or in a mixture or in a bread recipe, remember to leave the shells in, too. Whirling a whole egg in the blender is an easy way to incorporate the shell when making birdy bread.

in its natural form, still on the stem, and birds go crazy for it.

New Foods

Birds, especially older ones, are sometimes reluctant to try new foods. If you are lucky, your bird will have been weaned onto a huge variety of foods, so it will be naturally inclined to try almost anything. The keys to getting an obstreperous bird to accept unfamiliar food items are persistence, patience, and perseverance. Especially stubborn are birds used to getting nothing but seeds, and there are cases where such birds had to be offered fresh foods on a daily basis for a year or more before they learned to eat a more healthy diet.

A very good way of enticing a hesitant bird is to allow it to see someone else eating the new food—either another bird, or you. Meals are a social event for lovebirds, and they are very likely to imitate if they see something being enjoyed.

Finch and canary seed mixes can provide a welcome treat for your lovebird.

The Common Species

There are three species of lovebird that show up in pet shops on a regular basis in the United States. The Peachfaced and the

Lovebirds can be mischievous and playful, and hand-raised birds make especially affectionate pets.

Masked are very common, and the Fischer's is fairly common. All three species make fine pets, and they come in a variety of colors, especially the Peachfaced Lovebird, which can be bred in hundreds of different combinations of mutations.

PEACHFACED LOVEBIRD

This is the largest species. The back of the Peachfaced Lovebird (*Agapornis roseicollis*) is dark green, with lighter green underneath. The flight feathers are black-edged, and the rump is a brilliant blue. The face is a beautiful orange-pink—the peach of the common name, and the forehead is red. The beak is light.

This is the most common lovebird in captivity. It is a free breeder, and there are more than a dozen mutations that have been established. Particularly striking is the Lutino Peachfaced, which is an overall bright yellow, with a red face. The dark factor, which also occurs in budgies, means

Consider the characteristics of different lovebirds before making a selection: personality, health, and cost can vary from bird to bird.

that many of the color types can occur in three phases—light, medium, and dark. The violet factor, also shared with budgies, modifies the feather structure so that a violet cast is given to the underlying color. It is interesting that the blue mutation, which is called the Dutch Blue, is an attractive greenish blue, not the sky blue of the blue budgie or of the masked lovebirds.

The list of established mutations is added to rather frequently, and they can be combined in thousands of varieties to produce all of the colors of Peachfaced lovebirds that you will find for sale. Some mutations are much rarer and more expensive, though the underlying birds are all the same.

Peachfaces of all colors are equally wonderful pets. They are active, daring, and amusing birds. When hand-raised, they are extremely affectionate and playful. They especially like dark, enclosed places, so don't be surprised if your pet disappears up your sleeve!

These little fellows are intelligent and aware, and even untamed birds will watch their owners and interact with them. They are brave to the point of often getting themselves into trouble, and like a young child, they have to be watched whenever they are out of their cage so that they do not get hurt and so they do not damage things around the house.

The Black-masked Lovebird has a large white eye-ring and a bright red beak; this species breeds freely and is available in a variety of mutations.

BLACK-MASKED LOVEBIRD

The Black-masked (*Agapornis personata*) is the second most common species in captivity, and it is often the same price or only slightly more than the Peachfaced. It is available in several mutations, the most common of which is the blue. This leads to confusion with naming. Technically, a blue morph of the normal green-with-black-face is a Blue Black-masked Lovebird. It is usually, however, called the Blue-masked Lovebird. The normal bird winds up being named for the color of its mask—black, while the blue bird is named for its body

color—blue. (There is no variety that has a blue mask.) In any case, it is a beautiful bird, having a clear, bright blue coloration with the black head. The yellow around the neck and throat is replaced with white. The normal green's beak is a deep, rich red color, which is considerably lightened in the blue phase. Incidentally, the Blue Masked was first found in the wild and did not arise in captive stocks, but was bred into them from wild blue imports.

This is one of the eye-ring lovebirds. There are four species in this group, according to most authorities. Older taxonomies called all four of these birds subspecies of the one species, *A. personata*. They are, however, four separate species. The problem lies in the fact that hybrids among these species are fertile, which not only leads to taxonomic

HYBRIDIZATION HAZARDS

Many species that do not cross breed in the wild will do so in captivity. Sometimes they simply do not live anywhere near each other but are easily brought together by bird breeders. Often they have some behavioral barriers to interbreeding, but in the unnatural confines of a cage and in the absence of a suitable mate of the same species, the birds will pair and breed. If we permit hybridization, we are contributing to the loss of these species as effectively as if we were killing off all the breeding stock. If future generations are going to be able to enjoy the natural beauty and charm of these little birds as they are found in the wild, we must avoid hybridization, which can turn captive stocks of these different species into one mongrelized group.

confusion, it also leads to a lot of mixed ancestry birds.

The Masked Lovebird makes an equally good pet as the Peachface. In my experience they are a bit less energetic than the Peachface—or rather, not quite as inclined to mischief, but I know other breeders who have found the opposite. In any case, a tame Masked can make an affectionate and delightful addition to your household.

FISCHER'S LOVEBIRD

Smaller than the Masked, the Fischer's Lovebird (*Agapornis fischeri*) is the other of the common eye-ring species. This bird is not as commonly available as the Peachfaced or Masked, but you should be able to find them with a little perseverance. This is another friendly species that makes an exceptional pet when hand raised. Some people claim that the eye-ring species have the sweetest personalities, but those are fighting words to a Peachface fan!

The bright green of the body is accented by bright red on the forehead. The beak is red. The top and back of the head have a dusky olive suffusion. The rump is violet, with any trace of gray

Established mutations of the common Peachfaced Lovebird include the Lutino (left) and the Pied Dutch Blue (right).

The blue variety of the Black-masked Lovebird is often called the Blue-masked Lovebird. The mask itself is black in both varieties.

indicating hybrid ancestry. Established color mutations include blue, white, yellow, and lutino. The "yellow" is an incomplete dilution and appears more as marbling of yellow and green. The blue is a pure blue, as in the Masked.

THE RARE SPECIES

The other six species of lovebirds are either rare in aviculture or completely absent, at least in the United States. Problems with viability are often encountered, with birds sometimes dying for no apparent reason as they mature. Even when healthy adults are obtained, breeding is often problematic, and often few, if any of the young produced survive. Dedicated breeders are working with some of these birds, however, and it is possible that the future will be brighter

for us being able to keep these birds easily in captivity.

You are unlikely to encounter any of these birds, and if you do, their price will probably scare you off. Nevertheless, I include them here for completeness, and also because you may very well become "hooked" on lovebirds and go on to breed them. In this case, you may be one of those people who will contribute to the establishment of these rare species in captivity.

Nyasa Lovebird (*Agapornis lilianae*)

These first two species complete the eye-ring group, which also includes the Masked and Fischer's. The Nyasa is only about 5 inches long and is much more slender and fine-featured than the Masked or Fischer's. Its green body is accented by a reddish orange head. The tail has an orange and black band. The beak fades from a red tip to a light pink. A great deal of hybridizing has occurred in this species. You should suspect birds if they do not have the delicate body type, or if they have large bills, or red bills, because the red beak of the Masked and Fischer's predominates in the hybrid offspring. Any blue color in the rump indicates hybrid origin, while a dark green rump is a sign of hybridization with Black-Cheeks. Any black on the face is also an indication of hybrid ancestry.

Black-Cheeked Lovebird
(*Agapornis nigrigenis*)

This eye-ring lovebird is, of course, mostly green. It has a brownish-black face and cheeks, but the back of the head is a dark, sooty bronze. There is an orange bib on the throat, and the breast is olive green, as is the rump, which in purebred birds has no blue at all.

This bird is not only rare in captivity, but it is endangered in the wild as well. Loss of habitat, especially water sources, is especially threatening because of this species' limited natural range. Some sources indicate that this is Africa's most endangered parrot. Captive populations are slowly increasing, so there is hope that domestic strains of Black-Cheeks will eventually be well established. Despite its rarity, there are a few color mutations of this species, though unfortunate hybridizing has taken place. You can detect signs of hybridization by looking for red on the head (from hybrids with Nyasa or Fischer's), or excessive black on

the head (from crosses with Masked). In addition, the rump must be free of any blue feathering.

Madagascar Lovebird
(*Agapornis cana*)

The next three species listed here are the sexually dimorphic species—males and females are colored differently. In the Madagascar, the hen is a bright green. The male has a gray head, neck, and breast, and black on the underside of the wings. The female Madagascar Lovebird carries strips of nesting material tucked among

With its white eye ring, red beak, and vivid green body, the Fischer's Lovebird is an attractive and relatively common species.

When selecting a lovebird from a breeder or dealer, seek out only the healthiest birds; look for excellent feather condition, clear eyes, and steady breathing.

the feathers of both breast and rump.

This species is very rare in aviculture, and it is important that all specimens be in active breeding programs so that they can become firmly established. Unfortunately, almost any animal native to Madagascar is either extinct or threatened with extinction, because the rapid development of this growing island nation has been very hard on its wildlife.

Abyssinian Lovebird
(*Agapornis taranta*)

In this species, the cock has red on its forehead and around its eyes, as well as black under the wings. The rest of the bird, and the entire female, is green. Both sexes have a red beak. Upon fledging, the babies are all green, but they can be sexed by the black on the wings, which the males already have at this age. It is several months more until the red coloration appears. The Abyssinian is longer than the Peachfaced—slightly more than 6.5 inches, but it is a more slender bird, so the Peachfaced seems larger.

This lovebird is native to mountain areas and is adapted to cooler temperatures. It lives in flocks but nests as separate pairs, and they cannot be colony bred. Although not common in captivity, there are some breeding populations, and a few color mutations have been developed.

Red-faced Lovebird (*Agapornis pullaria*)

This species is just about 6 inches long. The face of the cock is reddish orange, with black under the wings. There is a red and black band on the tail, and the bill is red. The rump is blue. The hen is a paler version, lacking the black on the wings, and having only pale orange on the head.

These birds have proven quite difficult to keep, and even harder to breed in captivity. In the wild they nest in burrows they excavate in ant nests or termite mounds. These structures have remarkable thermal insulation capacities, enabling the hen to leave the eggs for much longer periods than would be possible otherwise, and this

As with the Blue Black-masked Lovebird, the Blue Fischer's is a pure blue mutation.

The Peachfaced, Masked, and Fischer's are the most commonly found species.

may account for much of the breeding difficulty aviculturists have encountered. A few mutations have been reported, but there is not even a stable population of the wild-type birds breeding in captivity.

Black-Collared Lovebird (*Agapornis swindernia*)

This last is not obviously allied to any other species, though some group it with the Peachfaced. I can find no reference to its being kept in captivity, either in the United States or in Europe, and I have never seen one. These birds live in tropical rainforests and must be trapped in the canopy. Once caught, they have proved impossible to keep alive, probably because of special dietary needs. There is a story of their being kept alive by an African aviculturist on a diet of fresh figs.

Colored Peachies

Color mutations are known in many parrot species, but only three species have exceptional variety in color types. Budgies (the common "parakeet"), Indian Ringnecks, and Peachfaced Lovebirds have many established mutations, and with combinations of mutations, hundreds or even thousands of different types of birds are possible. Of course, many of these different genetic types look the same as each other; for example, pied, which removes melanin (dark pigment) from splotches all over the bird, and lutino, which removes all melanin from anywhere on the bird, can be combined in the same bird, which will not be any different in appearance than a non-pied lutino. Then again, some combinations are not considered particularly attractive and are therefore not propagated, though there tend to be trends and fads in this regard. Also, when dealing with multiple mutations in a single bird, it may not be possible to visually determine the bird's genetic makeup, and test breedings may be necessary to know exactly what mutations the bird actually carries. Especially confusing are the dark and

Like budgerigars, the different genetic types of Peachfaced Lovebirds can be combined in thousands of ways.

violet factors, which in their various combinations can be very difficult to recognize and/or differentiate.

When a new mutation first appears, birds showing this trait are extremely expensive, and there is a rush to breed them. Soon the "gold rush" is over, and the birds command more normal prices and are widely available. Many of the colors have country names in their names; these reflect the country of origin. For example, two different genes for cinnamon have arisen, one in the United States and one in Australia. They are therefore called American cinnamon and Australian cinnamon.

Since many of the colors of Peachfaced Lovebirds are regularly available, and because there is such diversity, this chapter is devoted to the color varieties of Peachfaced Lovebirds and will introduce you to them and to the genetics behind them.

COLORS VERSUS PIGMENTS

Although it appears that a white lovebird is colored white, and a blue one blue, and a yellow one yellow, and a green one green, this is not the case. Color in birds has at least two different origins—pigments and feather structure. There are only three color pigments in lovebirds—melanin (black or brown), red, and yellow. A normal wild-type Peachfaced has all three types. The red and yellow is obviously involved in the orange of the face, and the black flight feathers are obviously colored with

The normal Peachfaced has a reddish-pink forehead, throat, cheeks, chin, and upper abdomen.

THE GUIDE TO OWNING A LOVEBIRD

Cobalt and Pastel Blue Lovebirds.

melanin, but what about the green body and the blue rump?

Well, the rump feathers are colored with melanin, but the feather structure is modified so that blue light is reflected. There is no blue coloring in the feathers, but they reflect blue light and are therefore seen as blue. The same is true for the body feathers, only they also have yellow pigment in them, so they appear green. Therefore, it stands to reason that if you remove the melanin from a green feather, it should appear yellow, and that, in fact, is the case; a lutino Peachfaced has a bright yellow body, with a red-orange face, and white flight feathers.

A BIT OF GENETICS

We need to define just a few terms in order to be able to discuss the color varieties of Peachfaced Lovebirds. As you probably know, genes are found on chromosomes, and each species has a specific number of chromosomes, which occur in pairs. An animal gets one chromosome of each pair from each parent. It therefore gets one gene for a given trait from each parent.

Blue Pied Lovebird, with the pied mutation characterized by irregular patches of whitened plumage.

If the two genes are the same (either both for the wild-type trait or both for the same mutation), we say the animal is pure or homozygous for that trait. If they are not the same, we say the animal is split or heterozygous for that trait. But what trait is expressed when the animal is heterozygous?

There are basically three possibilities, and we can illustrate each of them with actual examples. For all three we will consider an animal that got a gene for the wild-type trait from one parent and for a particular mutation from the other parent.

Recessive Mutation

We can illustrate this with human eye color (for this example we will restrict our observations of eye colors to just blue and brown). Blue eye color is a recessive mutation, which means that it will only be expressed when found in the pure or homozygous state. A person with one gene for blue eyes and one for brown eyes will have brown eyes. Their brown eyes will look just like those of a person with two genes for brown eyes. The heterozygous or split person, however, will pass the blue eye gene on to half of his or her offspring—to those that receive the chromosome with the blue gene on it. This means that if the other parent is blue-eyed, or if the other parent is also split—brown-eyed but carrying the gene for blue eyes—then they can have a baby with blue eyes. A person with two genes for brown eyes, however, cannot have a blue-eyed baby even if the other parent has blue eyes, because all the children will get a brown gene.

Dominant Mutation

We'll use cats for this example. In cats, white fur is a dominant mutation. No matter what color genes the cat has, if it has one gene for white fur, it will be a white cat. Of course, it will also be white if it has two genes for white. A white cat can therefore produce white kittens when paired with a cat of any color. If it has two white genes, all of its kittens will be white, no matter what color the other parent is, because no matter which chromosome it gives to a kitten, it will have a white gene on it. If it is heterozygous or split for white, and if it is mated to a cat of some other color, then some of the kittens will be white, and some will not be.

Co-dominant Mutation

Sometimes neither of two traits will be dominant over the other, and this is called partial dominance, incomplete dominance, or co-dominance. In this case, a heterozygous individual will be intermediate in appearance between the two traits. A good example of this is found in poultry with a color called blue, which is a bluish-gray color. This blue coloration is, in fact, the heterozygous condition, caused by a bird having one black gene and one silver gene. A bird with two black genes appears black, and one with two silver genes appears a silvery off-white or very light gray. When a bird inherits one black and one silver gene, it appears blue. Two blue birds mated together, then, produce chicks of all three colors—black, blue, and silver, depending on whether they get a black gene from each parent, a black from one parent and a silver from the other, or silver from both parents.

Another way of looking at co-dominance is as a cumulative effect. In this case, the black bird has normal melanin production. The blue mutation causes a dilution and diffusion of the melanin. In one "dose," it creates the blue color, but in the homozygous double dose, it produces the even more dilute and diffuse silver color.

SEX LINKAGE

One other condition is relevant to a discussion of lovebird genetics—sex linkage. You'll remember that sex in mammals is determined by the X and Y chromosomes. Women have two X's, and men have one X and one Y. Thus, every egg a woman produces has an X

The rump is an important area for identifying carried factors, but even experts may not be able to spot certain mutations.

chromosome in it, so everyone gets an X from their mother. Half of a man's sperm contain an X chromosome, and half contain a Y. When a child inherits the X chromosome from both mother and father, the child is a girl (X/X). When it gets a Y from its father, it is a boy (X/Y).

Sex determination in birds is similar, but reversed. A male bird has two like sex chromosomes, Z's, so a cock bird is Z/Z. A female bird has two different sex chromosomes, one Z and one W. Thus, it is the hen that determines the sex of the chicks, because every bird gets a Z from its father. If it also gets a Z from its mother, the chick is a male, but if it gets a W from its mother, the chick is a female.

Why is this important? Because many mutations are found on the Z chromosome. This means that a male bird carries two genes for these traits, while a female carries only one—on her Z chromosome. The W chromosome does not have any known mutations on it. In lovebirds, the lutino gene we mentioned above is sex-linked, meaning it is found on the Z chromosome. Remember that this gene removes all melanin from the bird, wherever it might occur, but leaves red and yellow pigments unaffected. The corresponding wild-type gene is for normal melanin production.

Let's label this gene "ino" and use it as a superscript to indicate the presence of this mutation on a Z chromosome: Z^{ino}. It is the practice to indicate the wild-type gene with a plus symbol, so we can denote a Z chromosome with the gene for normal melanin production by Z^{ino+}, or for simplicity, $Z+$. This gives us the following notations:

normal male $Z+ / Z+$

normal female $Z+ / W$

lutino male Z^{ino} / Z^{ino}

lutino female Z^{ino} / W

normal male, split to lutino $Z+ / Z^{ino}$

Lutino is a recessive mutation, so if we cross a normal cock bird with a lutino hen, we get the following:

normal cock   x   lutino hen

$Z+ / Z+$ x Z^{ino} / W

This produces:

male chicks that are normally colored but split for lutino

$Z+ / Z^{ino}$

and female chicks that are normal and do not carry lutino

$Z+ / W$

Notice that if we set up the opposite pair, a lutino cock and a normal hen, the results are quite different:

lutino cock   x   normal hen

Z^{ino} / Z^{ino} x $Z+ / W$

Since each chick gets the lutino gene from its father, this produces:

male chicks that are normally colored but split for lutino

$Z+ / Z^{ino}$

but female chicks that are all lutino!

Z^{ino} / W

This is a very popular mating with sex-linked mutations—a visual male (with two genes for the trait) and a normal female (with one wild-type gene only). The chicks can be sexed by color—the males are normal and the females show the mutation, but all of the males are guaranteed split for the trait.

Notice that only cock birds can be split for lutino. Since a hen has only one Z, she either has the gene for normal melanin or she has one for lutino. A cock, however, can have both genes, one on each Z chromosome. Such a bird, Z+ / Zino, is visually normal, but it carries the lutino gene and will pass it on to half of his offspring. With non sex-linked mutations, of course, both males and females can be split for the trait.

RECESSIVE PEACHFACED MUTATIONS

There are several recognized recessive mutations. These are not sex-linked, and split birds appear normal.

The Blues

There are two blue mutations in Peachfaces, the Dutch blue (DB) and the white-faced blue (WFB). These are both mutations of the gene for normal red and yellow pigment production. The DB gene removes a lot of these pigments. A bird homozygous for this gene (DB/DB) has a body that is greenish blue, with a creamy orange face. The red band on the forehead is replaced with orange.

The WFB gene removes even more of the pigments, but still not all, so a bird homozygous for this gene (WFB/WFB) has a white face, and there is usually still some faint orange coloration on the forehead.

Since both of these are mutations of the same wild-type gene, a bird can only have a total of two of them, one on each

The orange-face mutation can vary from bird to bird, with differing amounts of orange coloration in the face.

chromosome. Thus, the possible combinations are:

Two wild-type genes (+/+)—this bird is normal green.

One wild-type and one DB (+/DB)—this bird is normal green, but split for DB.

One wild-type and one WFB (+/WFB)—this bird is normal green, but split for WFB.

Two DB's (DB/DB)—this bird is a Dutch blue.

Two WFB's (WFB/WFB)—this bird is a whiteface blue.

Or one of each mutation (DB/WFB)—this bird is called a seagreen. The seagreen

Lutino combines in interesting ways with the various blue mutations.

looks a great deal like a Dutch blue, but its body color is much greener.

Ino Blues

As stated above, the pure blue mutation has not yet appeared in Peachfaced Lovebirds. All three blue types, Dutch blue, whiteface, and seagreen, result from an incomplete elimination of red and yellow pigments. Therefore, their combination with the Ino gene, which produces lutinos in otherwise green birds and when combined with a true blue mutation produces albinos, does not produce true albinos in Peachfaces. Dutch blue combined with lutino produces the creamino, which is a creamy yellow bird. The WFB lutino is sometimes called an albino, and it is much whiter than the creamino, but it still shows some yellow pigmentation.

Orange Face

The orange face mutation (OF) has only been around since the late 1980s. A bird homozygous for orange face (OF/OF) has much of the red removed from the face, leaving a true orange rather than the reddish orange of the wild type bird. In addition, the body is a slightly lighter shade of green. There is considerable individual variation in the amount of orange, and often a split individual (+/OF) will show a bit more orange in its face than a normal Peachface.

American Yellow

The American yellow mutation (AY), sometimes called "cherryhead," is a dilution of the melanin, rather than a complete removal as in the lutino. The birds appear greenish yellow, with a light blue rump. A scalloped or "penciled" appearance is caused by a faint dark edging on each individual feather.

When a bird is homozygous for both American yellow and Dutch blue (AY/AY DB/DB) it is light gray in color, with a very pale blue rump. These are called "white" or "silver," and with the penciling on the feathers, they can be very attractive birds.

Australian Pied

This is a recessive pied, also known as dark-eyed clear because it removes melanin from the feathers but leaves the eye dark, not red as in the lutino. The amount of pied markings is variable.

DOMINANT PEACHFACED MUTATION
American Pied

The only known dominant mutation is the American Pied. It acts to remove melanin, but only in irregular patches, not over the entire bird. The position, size, and number of these yellow or yellow-green patches is extremely variable, and a pied bird can range from normal-looking all the way to almost completely yellow. Usually pairing heavily pied birds will produce heavily pied offspring, but not always, and a bird that was thought to be normal because of scant expression of the gene can throw markedly pied offspring.

When a blue bird is also pied, the splotches, of course, appear yellow-white rather than yellow. In all cases the effect of this gene looks rather like the birds had bleach spilled on their feathers, causing irregular whitening. Some pied birds are very beautiful, but depending on their markings, they can also look blotchy.

SEX-LINKED PEACHFACED MUTATIONS

We've already discussed the most common sex-linked color—lutino. There are two mutations called cinnamon (sometimes called "fallow"), which are sex-linked—American cinnamon and Australian cinnamon. Both of these genes work to partially remove or dilute melanin, so the result is a yellowing of the normal green.

For many, the appeal of lovebirds lies in the ease with which a breeder can experiment with colors and mutations.

Certain breeding combinations can produce odd results; fortunately, this young Green Pied Lovebird has unusual but attractive markings.

The American cinnamon is the darker bird, best described as a light green, with gray rather than black flight feathers. The Australian cinnamon gene removes more melanin, but still less than the total removal of lutino, so the bird appears a very light greenish yellow, intermediate between an American cinnamon and a lutino. Both types of cinnamon have red eyes as chicks, but they darken with age to look normal.

CO-DOMINANT PEACHFACED MUTATIONS

There are three co-dominant or cumulative mutations.

Dark Factor

The dark factor is known in many parrot species. It does not change the pigments present but instead changes the amount of light reflected by the feathers, creating deeper, darker shades. A normal wild-type bird has no dark factors and can be thought of as "light." Birds can have either one or two dark factors,

New color combinations are constantly being developed; pictured is the Mauve Lovebird.

THE GUIDE TO OWNING A LOVEBIRD

which produce "medium" and "dark" varieties, respectively.

Many names are confused together around the dark factor. Medium green is called "jade," dark green "olive," medium blue "cobalt," and dark blue "slate." In essence, any melanin-related color of Peachfaced Lovebird can be produced in three shades: light, medium, and dark.

In the normal green series, the medium (jade) green has a deeper green coloration and a navy blue (rather than turquoise) rump. The dark green (olive) has olive-green color with a slate gray rump. Sometimes when many mutations are combined, it is difficult to be sure how many dark factors, if any, a bird is carrying.

The Violets

The two violet mutations, like the dark factor, affect not pigment but feather structure. They cause more violet light to be reflected, giving a purplish cast to the bird. Since it is cumulative, a single violet factor bird will show less violet coloration than a double factor bird. When a single dark factor is combined with violet, it increases the violet color. Double dark violet birds, however, often look little different from plain double darks, because there is so little light reflected that the violet does not come through.

The American violet mutation appeared first, but it produces a much more subtle violet color, and the Danish violet mutation from the late 1980s is much more popular. Danish violet is especially beautiful on a whiteface blue, producing a

The dark factor affects the amount of light reflected by feathers but not the pigment itself. Pictured is a dark green or "olive" baby bird, whose red face will deepen with age.

bird that is an overall violet with a rich purple rump. It is also quite beautiful combined with Australian cinnamon. The American violet, when combined on an Australian cinnamon blue bird, produces a pale lilac or orchid color.

NEW MUTATIONS

As you can see, the many color mutations can combine in many interesting ways. Some of the colors have been around for a long time, and a few are less than 10 years old. Certainly there will be more mutations in the future.

Breeding

Even though you may feel that all you want is one lovebird as a pet, you may find that some time down the road you will want to collect several lovebirds, and you might want to try breeding them. Part of the sustained appeal of lovebirds is their availability and low price, which in turn are due to their free breeding in captivity.

SELECTING YOUR BREEDING STOCK

Obviously you want large, healthy, robust birds as breeders—birds that demonstrate the proper coloration and configuration for the type they are, and, of course, you should make sure that you only pair up birds of the same species. It is best to pair unrelated birds, though some inbreeding is acceptable, especially when you are

The availability of relatively inexpensive lovebirds has encouraged the efforts of hobbyist breeders.

Two lovebirds do not necessarily equal a breeding pair; compatibility may be more likely if birds are allowed to choose their own mates.

trying to establish specific mutations. Often breeders trade like lovebirds in order to bring new bloodlines of the same color varieties into their stock. But how do you select which birds to pair up?

PAIRING

The best way to ensure success is to allow the birds to pair naturally. It is not the case that a male lovebird and a female lovebird equals a pair. Some birds simply do not get along, and often when birds choose their own mates, the pairs are much more stable and likely to breed successfully. If you have sufficient of the appropriate color, you can put all the birds together in a large flight and then watch for obvious signs of pair bonding—sitting together, feeding and preening each other, keeping other birds away.

But let's say you only want one pair. Because the three common species are all non-dimorphic, meaning the sexes look alike, there are only three sure ways of getting a true pair.

Proven Pairs

You can buy a proven pair, meaning that they have produced babies with each other. Not only do you know they are male and female, but you know they are compatible. This depends completely on the honesty of the seller, however. I wish I had a dollar for every "proven pair" a breeder bought only to find out they were two of the same sex! If you decide to go this route, get a guarantee in writing,

The proper nest box set up—with an enclosed box and plenty of nesting material—is critical to breeding success.

which any reputable breeder will be more than happy to provide. You can buy proven singles as well, meaning the birds have produced babies and are of known sex. If you get a proven male and a proven female, you will not have to worry about having two of the same sex, but there still could be incompatibility problems.

DNA Sexing

DNA sexing has become very popular, since it requires only a small drop of blood. The sample is obtained either from a pinprick or from the base of a plucked feather. It is then sent to a laboratory, where the blood is analyzed and the sex is determined. A certificate verifying the sex of the bird and its closed band number is then provided. Mistakes are possible as with any type of blood testing, but they are very rare and are usually clerical in nature.

Surgical Sexing

Surgical sexing is a procedure performed by a veterinarian while the bird is anesthetized. A small incision is made, and the interior organs of the bird are examined laproscopically with tiny imaging devices inserted through the incision. Not only can the doctor identify the bird's sex, he or she can examine the overall health of the bird and of the reproductive system. It is typical for the bird to be permanently tattooed at the same time, and valuable birds are usually microchipped as well to provide permanent, unalterable identification.

Any other method of selecting a pair, such as feeling the distance between the vent bones or observing behavior, runs the risk of producing two birds of the same sex. Of course, just reaching blindfolded into a cage full of birds and grabbing the first two you hit has a fifty-fifty chance of producing a male and a female.

COLOR MATCHING

A male lovebird of any color can mate successfully with a female lovebird of the same species of any color. Not all matches, however, are equally useful or productive. For example, you might think that pairing a Dutch blue to an American yellow will produce silvers (American yellow blues). It won't. All the chicks will be normal greens. This is because each bird carries two wild-type genes for the other's trait. The blue is really B/B Y+/Y+, and the yellow is B+/B+ Y/Y. All of the chicks, therefore, will be split for both traits (B+/B Y+/Y) but will appear as normal green Peachfaces.

If two such split birds are mated, the chicks can include normal greens, Dutch blues, and American yellows, along with the desired yellow-blues or silvers, although you would have to have many clutches raised before you got one. It is important to realize that some of the birds will be splits, but some will not. If you did enough matings, you would get a ratio among four visual types: 9 normals to 3 blues to 3 yellows to 1 silver.

There are actually nine different genetic makeups among these four color types in the offspring, even though several look the same. With sufficient numbers to get an accurate manifestation of the genetic possibilities, this generation will include, for every 16 chicks:

1 blue (not split to yellow)

1 yellow (not split to blue)

1 normal green (not split to blue or to yellow)

1 blue-yellow (silver)

2 normal green split to blue (and not to yellow)

2 normal green split to yellow (and not to blue)

2 yellow split to blue

2 blue split to yellow

and 4 green split to blue and to yellow.

Limiting a cage to one pair will help to eliminate the potential distractions and squabbling found in groups of lovebirds.

You can see, then, that the nine greens contain birds split to blue, birds split to yellow, and split to both, but also one bird that does not carry either mutation but is pure wild-type. Likewise, the three blue birds contain two split to yellow but one that does not carry that trait, and the three yellow birds include two split to blue but one that is not. There is no way to determine which birds are split and which are not except through test matings.

For this reason, breeding split to split is not a preferred pairing. It is always best to mate a split bird to a visual, meaning that the split's mate should exhibit the traits it is split for. The offspring of such a mating will always be visuals and splits, but there will be no pure wild-type birds. Dominant and sex-linked mutations complicate matters even further. When you consider pairing birds that each have multiple mutations, it requires a good understanding of the genetics involved just to figure out what the pairing can produce. If you get to the point of wanting to work with these color types, you will undoubtedly spend a lot of time studying lovebird genetics, so you don't have to worry about it now. There is no pairing that is "wrong," so that even an unproductive mating of two rare colors that produces all normal-looking chicks is perfectly valid. It is simply the case that without proper planning, two expensive birds may be paired only to produce all normal green babies that are much less valuable. Of course, sometimes two birds you believe to be normal greens both turn out to be split for some trait or traits, and you get pleasant surprises in the babies. The only pairings absolutely to avoid are of birds of different species; you should not jeopardize the integrity of captive bloodlines by hybridizing.

Although colony breeding is a viable method with lovebirds, cage breeding allows you to work with and keep track of mutations.

THE GUIDE TO OWNING A LOVEBIRD

HOUSING YOUR BREEDERS

A cage for breeding lovebirds does not need to be very different from a regular cage. Since two birds are involved, it should be roomy, and it will need a provision for attaching a nest box. Normally the box is fitted to the outside of the cage, and the birds access the nest hole through a door or other opening in the side of the cage. This makes it much easier for you to check on the nest. Not all lovebird breeders use one-pair cages, however.

Cage or Colony?

Sometimes lovebirds are bred by the colony system, where a number of pairs are placed together in a large aviary with many more nest boxes than there are pairs, to reduce fighting over choice locations. The number of pairs included depends on the size of the aviary. Results are often favorable, but there can be problems with this method. Only the eye-ring species can be bred this way, but Peachfaces should not be. They are not communal breeders in the wild, and they usually will not tolerate other breeders in the same enclosure. The death of some of the breeders and of any chicks that are produced is the likely result. And although harmony is much more likely with the eye-ring species, such problems can also arise with them.

If you decide to colony breed, it is very important to provide plenty of nesting sites, preferably all at the same height. With an abundance of choices that all

A budgie-size nest box will suffice for most lovebirds, but a slightly larger box is preferred.

offer the same advantages, there will be much less squabbling over any particular box.

It is essential that you make sure you have an equal number of males and females, since unpaired birds can cause problems for the nesting pairs. It is even better if you introduce the birds after they have paired. This way they are likely to remain in the original pairs, and problems with courtship and competition for mates is avoided.

The feeders and waterers must be adequate, and numerous enough so that meeker birds will not be kept away from food and water. In my opinion, colony breeding can be very rewarding, but it is almost always a better idea to use

Although new or unusual color variations will raise the price of a lovebird, Peachfaced and common variations are generally inexpensive.

individual cages for the pairs for a variety of reasons.

Breeding Success

In a colony situation, there are a number of social dynamics that the birds have to contend with, from feeding to defense of territory. These amount to a lot of distractions and additional worries for the breeding birds. In separate cages, the birds can concentrate on hatching and raising their babies without having to interact with other pairs except vocally—which they will do!

It is also much easier for you to monitor progress and change with cages. Checking the nest boxes, banding babies, and keeping track of each pair is greatly simplified when there is only one pair per cage. When you have several pairs breeding at the same time and they have widely differing numbers of eggs, you can foster eggs or chicks from the crowded nests into the emptier nests, and this is much easier to accomplish with cages as well.

Pedigree

Although lovebird pairs are normally faithful to each other, there are occasions when they are not, and the parentage of a bird produced in a colony can never be certain. You cannot even be sure of who the mother is, since on occasion a hen will lay an egg in another pair's nest, or she will be evicted from her own nest after laying some eggs, which may be taken over by the newcomers rather than tossed out.

AGGRESSION

Even with only one pair to a cage you may get fighting, injuries, and even spousicide, but you obviously will not have to contend with disagreements between different pairs. While some lovebird parents that are already starting a second clutch can be quite aggressive toward their first clutch of chicks when they fledge, this is easy to detect in a cage situation, and the young can be removed to safety. In a colony setup, newly-fledged birds can be severely abused by any of the adults present. Isolating each pair in its own cage can also increase breeding success.

You might think that if you only put birds of one color type in a colony that this is not a concern, but if any of the birds are split for other traits, colony breeding can louse up your records considerably.

Nest Boxes

Being cavity nesters, lovebirds require an enclosed nest box. They will use a standard budgie nest box, but they prefer a slightly larger box, since they often use considerable nesting material and fill the box quite full. Many breeders find that a horizontal rather than a vertical box is preferable, and with the rare species, which are often difficult to induce to breed, various attempts at providing more natural nest sites are made, including using sections of actual hollow logs.

FEEDING AND BREEDING

Feeding and breeding are closely related. Once an egg is laid, the parents can only give the chick heat and moisture. All of the nutrition in the egg has to be provided by the mother in the weeks before it is laid. Dietary inadequacies are behind weak chicks, dead-in-the-shell chicks, thin shells that break, and other breeding problems. In addition, poor nutrition of the breeders can contribute to infertility.

Once the chicks hatch, the only food they get is what the parents bring to them, and that, ultimately, comes from what you feed the breeders. The regular daily diet of your lovebirds should already be varied and balanced, but during breeding you should pay special attention to fresh fruits and vegetables,

A plentiful supply of clean nesting material should be provided to lovebirds at the start of the breeding season.

Nest boxes can be fitted to a cage to allow keepers to monitor the nest and the progress of the eggs.

Baby lovebirds that are handfed are generally tamer than those that are parent-raised, but the task is extremely difficult and requires a serious commitment.

and extra eggs and soft foods. The latter are especially important when the birds are feeding young.

A BREEDING CALENDAR

Most lovebirds will breed year-round, though some show a definite breeding season. Some pairs will raise two or three clutches and take a break, others will keep on breeding. It is too taxing on the birds to have more than three broods in a row, and two is better.

A good schedule to follow is to put up the nest boxes in the spring, allow them to raise two to three clutches, then remove the nest boxes for a winter rest. During this rest period it is fine to place all of your breeders together in a large flight cage or aviary. If they are banded, you will have no problem separating out the pairs again in the spring. You can even mix species, though in that case you have to be even more attentive to possible aggression problems. When they are not breeding, lovebirds of all species usually get along, but not always.

HANDFEEDING THE BABIES

If you wish to learn to hand-feed babies, you should enlist the aid of an experienced breeder. You might be able to trade handfeeding lessons for help with chores. Although an enjoyable task, handfeeding a large number of baby birds can be quite tedious and nerve-wracking. Many breeders would welcome the chance to have an "apprentice" help out for a while.

I am giving no instructions here because I do not feel that inexperienced people should undertake this task without a lot of training. The actual process of getting the food into the chick is not difficult to master, but knowing how to spot medical

Adults starting their second clutch of chicks may be aggressive toward their first clutch, and they should be watched carefully.

Babies hatch on successive days, so a clutch will consist of babies of various ages and sizes.

problems before they get too serious is not something you can learn from a few paragraphs in a book. By spending time with an experienced handfeeder you will pick up the information that you need to raise healthy babies.

Taming and Training

Have you ever seen a bird show, with trained parrots performing tricks such as roller-skating, fetching objects, or doing athletic stunts? Well, lovebirds can also be trained to do some of these things. Many bird owners prefer a more "natural" relationship with their pets, and the birds themselves will invent their own tricks for your pleasure (and occasional displeasure, too!). The basis for training a bird is the trust and affection you must build up, which you will want even if you do not wish to teach it to do tricks on command.

TAMING AND HANDFEEDING

Although there are exceptions, generally you need to get a handfed bird in order to have a tame pet. Handfed birds are taken from the nest at a young age (sometimes at hatching). Such birds have no fear of being handled and are bonded to human beings. They make affectionate pets.

The level of training that you pursue with your lovebird is up to you, but even a minimal amount of taming and training can help build a trusting relationship.

It's best to buy a young bird soon after it has been weaned, when it will best be able to bond with you.

There are many problems that can arise during handfeeding, and it should only be undertaken by trained professionals, so you should get a bird that has been fed by the breeder until weaning.

You should buy your bird shortly after it is weaned—meaning that it is eating completely on its own. At this point in its life, a young lovebird is ready to form life-long bonds, and you will be getting it while it is eager to learn and free of bad habits.

If you get only one lovebird, it will make you its "flock." Two or more birds, even if hand-raised, will also form bonds with each other. Although mated pairs of lovebirds do spend a lot of time preening and feeding each other, this is also normal social behavior, and two males or two females can become close friends.

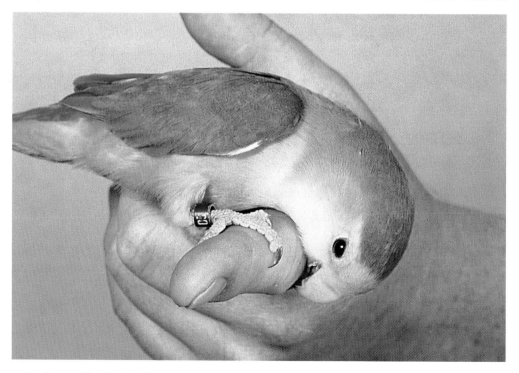

A hand-tamed lovebird will be comfortable stepping up to your hand, perhaps on command.

I'm not saying that you can't have more than one bird as a pet, only that a single bird will be more dependent on you for friendship and attention.

This is an important point. Owning a single, hand-raised lovebird requires a substantial commitment of time. These friendly and intelligent birds need a lot of attention, and taking care of their physical needs is only part of the required care. If you want a hand-tame pet but do not have that much time to commit, buying two hand-tame birds is a solution. This way you will be able to take them out and play with them, but they will have each other at other times.

A handfed bird will not automatically remain hand-tame. If it is simply placed in a cage with other birds and left for several months, it will need a lot of working with to regain its trust.

Treats such as millet spray can be used as rewards during training—head scratches and words of encouragement also work.

Training should be fun, so try to fit short, frequent sessions into your daily routine.

TRAINING

Whether you are trying to train your bird to stay off the kitchen counter or to ride a toy scooter, you must use patience and rewards, not discipline. Not all rewards have to be treats—a head scratching and words of praise will also reward your bird for a job well done. Break the desired behavior down into cumulative steps, and work on them one at a time.

You may be surprised to find that as your bird figures out what is going on, it might even anticipate behavior, and it will certainly learn new ones more quickly. By choosing behaviors that are an extension of the bird's natural repertoire, you will make training into a game, enjoyable for both of you. For example, it is natural for a lovebird to crack seeds open and remove the treat inside. If you want to train it to remove a treat from a tiny garbage can by removing the lid, it might be enough training simply to let him see you put the treat into the can—figuring out how to open it and get the treat won't be too difficult for the bird, even if you don't demonstrate the behavior.

For more complicated tasks, simply build up the behavior in small increments, making each part fun for the bird to learn. It is also important to constantly review tricks already learned so that the behavior remains fresh in the bird's mind. The most important thing to remember is that the whole idea of training your bird is to have fun. If any particular segment becomes tiresome for you or for your pet, try altering things until the spirit of enjoyment returns to the task at hand.

All of this applies to a regular "house rules" type of training. Your bird can learn that certain behaviors are inappropriate, and that certain ones are expected. It is especially important to think of the ramifications of anything you teach your pet or that it teaches itself. For example, it might seem cute to permit the bird to fly to the dinner table, check out each plate, and help itself to anything that looks tempting. Aside from the fact that the bird might eat things it shouldn't, think about how your boss or mother-in-law or best friend would feel if the bird did these things while they were dining with you. It is not difficult to train a lovebird to do something, but it can be very difficult to untrain it!

Health Care

This chapter is not going to be a compendium of symptoms, diagnoses, and treatments for all known avian diseases. First of all, that's way beyond the scope of this introductory book, and there are already fine treatments of this material written by experienced avian veterinarians. But the main reason I am not going to give that type of information is that it is extremely difficult, even for experienced bird owners, to identify and treat bird diseases. Usually a veterinary examination with blood and other laboratory tests is necessary to diagnose the problem.

Not only can birds not tell you what's wrong with them, there are only a few recognizable symptoms for all bird ailments. Unusual droppings, sitting puffed up and listless, respiratory noises such as coughs, sneezes, or wheezing, and loss of appetite are about the whole range. These are all associated with

A healthy lovebird can live for 10, even 20, years if it is fed a nutritious diet, given routine checkups, and allowed to exercise.

For its own safety, a bird that is allowed out of its cage should have its wings clipped, even if it is trained.

returns to normal. If your pet dive-bombed into a bag of flour and came out sneezing and shaking dust out of its feathers, it's obviously a safe bet that once it clears the dust from its nose, it will be all right.

GET A VET

Finding an avian veterinarian is absolutely essential as part of the care of your lovebird. Besides regular checkups, the veterinarian will be available if and when something serious happens to your bird. Please note that many dog and cat veterinarians are not trained in bird diseases and treatment. Even many poultry doctors are unable to provide complete care for parrots, which are medically quite different from the gallinaceous birds found on poultry farms.

Most larger cities, especially those with a school of veterinary medicine nearby, will have a doctor who specializes in exotic birds. Aside from being able to

enough serious problems that they warrant a trip to the veterinarian, at least the first time.

Of course, if there is an obvious reason for the symptom, you should first eliminate the reason and see if the symptom disappears. If your bird has loose, purplish stools, but you fed it blueberries that morning, well, it's a good idea to wait a day and see if they return to normal. If a puffed-up bird is wet or in a draft, put it in a warm place or place a heat lamp near its cage, and see if it

A NON-STICK WARNING

One of the most common tragedies among pet birds is poisoning from non-stick cookware. The coating on these pans, polytetrafluoroethylene (PTFE), when heated to about 500° F, emits a gas that kills birds instantly. Many bird owners have left a pan on the stove, which boiled dry, and returned a few minutes later to find all of their birds dead. Obviously, birds in the kitchen are at most risk, but the fumes do travel throughout the house. PTFE is found also in such things as hair dryers and space heaters. It is best to keep any type of heater or cookware far away from your bird.

58

properly diagnose and treat psittacine ailments, these veterinarians can offer guidance and advice with issues such as training, feeding, and breeding. If there is a zoo nearby, the veterinarians associated with it may be able to refer you to a colleague in private practice.

HOUSEHOLD POISONS

Most if not all cleansers, disinfectants, and other household chemicals are poisonous to birds and should not be used around them. Especially dangerous are chemicals designed to kill insects.

Many common houseplants are also toxic, not only to birds, but to all animals, including humans. Ivy, poinsettia, mistletoe, and dieffenbachia are among them, but it is best to consider any houseplant poisonous unless you are certain it is not. In any case, you don't want your lovebird chewing up your houseplants, so keep them separated.

ROUTINE CARE

There are several routine procedures for which you do not have to take your bird to the vet, though you will probably want either your vet or an experienced bird owner to demonstrate them first.

Nail Clipping

If they are not worn down with use, a bird's toenails will grow too long, which will interfere with its ability to get around and could prove dangerous if they get caught and entangled in something. Use a sharp nail clipper to cut the excess nail off. The only concern in clipping the nails

is that you avoid the quick—the blood vessel deep within the nail. Many lovebirds have dark nails, making it difficult to see this. Sometimes holding the nail up to a bright light will expose the vein, but if you cannot see it, simply cut the nail well above where you figure the blood vessel to be, then take very small snips until the nail looks normal. If you should hit the vein, you will not be very deep into it, and a dab with a styptic pencil should stop any bleeding. Remember what the nail looks like at that point, and always trim just a little longer in the future.

Wing Clipping

Wing clipping is a controversial topic—some people consider it absolutely essential, while others condemn it as

A lovebird that is accustomed to being handled will be less stressed when it must be held for examinations or grooming.

Treats such as millet spray should be given only occasionally and always in addition to a varied and nutritious diet.

mutilation. As with most such emotional issues, the truth lies in between the two extremes. Obviously a clipped bird cannot fly out the window, but it quite likely could escape out an open window anyway. A clipped bird will usually stay on a play gym until you come for it, although it is still able to jump off and flutter to the floor.

Many bird owners trim their bird's wings when they first get it but let the feathers grow back with the next molt. By that time it is tamed, trained, and accustomed to its new home. Lovebirds are such snugglebugs, however, that if your bird was hand raised, it will probably be so tame and bonded to humans that you will not need to clip its wings to control it or to be able to catch it to put it back in its cage when it is time.

If you decide to clip the wings, it is easiest to have the person you get it from show you how. The large flight feathers are cut with sharp scissors, straight across. You can leave the farthest most one or two feathers unclipped so that when the bird's wings are at rest they will look normal.

Beak Trimming

A lovebird's beak is constantly growing, but it usually stays in shape just from normal chewing behaviors. If, however, it begins to become overgrown, it will need to be trimmed back to its normal shape. Be extremely cautious; you only want to trim back the part that has grown too long. As long as the situation is not too bad, you may be able to file it back with an emery board. Just take it slow and remove only a little bit at a time.

INJURIES

It is not uncommon for lovebirds to get injured, unfortunately. Their curiosity, love of tight places, and fly-before-you-think impulsiveness often leads to cuts, scrapes, or bruises. Fortunately, birds have remarkable powers of recuperation and rarely do their wounds get infected. For superficial injuries, the same wash and disinfect routine you would use on yourself is perfectly adequate. Broken feathers should be gently but firmly plucked out by grabbing the base and tugging quickly. Left in, they will not be replaced until the next molt, but when pulled, a new feather will regrow in a couple of months.

More serious accidents can result in a broken wing or leg, which will be very obvious. Such injuries need prompt medical attention, and in most cases, when they are treated by a veterinarian, healing will be complete.

DISEASE

The biggest defense against disease in your lovebird is proper care. Clean living conditions, clean water and food vessels, and a nutritious, varied diet will go a long way to preventing any illness. If disease does strike, however, it is important that you take your bird to the veterinarian for an examination. Most birds do not show symptoms until a

Cleanliness is key to preventing illness, especially in a large collection where disease can spread quickly from bird to bird.

disease is well progressed, and time is of the essence. Many avian ailments are treatable when caught in time.

Probably the two most common problems veterinarians see in pet birds are chronic, long-term afflictions: obesity and liver disease. These are often related, but sometimes trim or even skinny birds have liver problems from an inadequate diet. Obesity is no more healthy for your bird than it is for you. Your lovebird will rely on you to monitor its food intake and to cut back on the high-calorie treats like sunflower seeds if it starts to get too hefty. When you first get your bird, you should feel its breastbone. Assuming the bird was properly raised, it will be in good shape, and the amount of flesh on its breast will be ideal. If later you find that the breastbone is more padded, put your pet on a low-cal diet, with plenty of fruits and vegetables. If you ever find your bird's breastbone is more prominent, indicating a weight loss, take it to the veterinarian immediately. A bird that is eating normally and losing weight needs prompt attention, as does a bird that is losing weight because it won't eat.

ENJOY!

You now have the knowledge you need to make an informed choice about whether a lovebird or two would be an appropriate addition to your family. If you decide that both you and the bird would benefit from the association, I am sure that it will be a long and pleasurable one. The love of a pet always brightens life a bit, but when that pet is as intelligent, curious, and affectionate as one of the African lovebirds, it is sure to become an ongoing source of enjoyment for you and your family.